A Woman
OF A Certain Age
Walks THE *Camino*

VÍA LÁCTEA

Copyright © 2013 by Ellen Waterston
All rights reserved.
Cover and book design by Atelier 6000
Cover art © Ron Schultz
Designed by Thomas Osborne

Atelier 6000 books are available at:
Atelier 6000
389 Scalehouse Court
Bend, Oregon 97702
Email: A6@atelier6000.org
Telephone: 541.330.8759

Founded in 2007, Atelier 6000 is a nonprofit studio specializing
in original prints and book arts. Support from private
foundations, corporate giving programs, government programs,
and generous individuals helps make the publication of our
books possible. We gratefully acknowledge their support.

Library of Congress Control Number 2013946831

ISBN 978-0-9893951-0-6 (ltd. edition art book alk.paper)
ISBN 978-0-9893951-1-3 (first edition/first printing alk. paper)
Printed in the United States of America

A version of "Clothes Line at the Hostel" appeared as "Line
Dried" in *Between Desert Seasons* by Ellen Waterston, Wordcraft
of Oregon, 2008. "November Sun–" appeared in *Between Desert
Seasons* by Ellen Waterston, Wordcraft of Oregon, 2008.

TO MY DEAR FRIEND KATHARINE BEAL DAVIS
WHO INSPIRED ME TO WALK THE *Camino de Santiago:*

To be on the pilgrim path trod for 1100 years calls me back again and again.

TO CRISTY LANFRI:

As I walked the Camino, profoundly aware that each of my footsteps was imprinting into thousands of footsteps that had come before, I felt a unique sense of unity with the other pilgrims. My wish is that this sense of unity happens more often in life, that we walk together peacefully and collaboratively towards common goals with such purity and grace.

TO LORETTA SLEPIKAS:

Fellow pilgrims along the way broke into my sacred silence ... but each was a blessing that changed me: Marc, a young German who made each step lighter with his humor; Victor, who appeared out of nowhere in a bright green poncho calling me, in his Indian accent, "beautiful young thing" (I'm 70) on one especially rainy day; and Paolo, from Italy, whose encouragement gave me hope. These individuals embody the spirit of the Camino. We are all on our own pilgrimages, together.

Table of Contents

Acknowledgments

I wish to thank the Oregon Arts Commission Career Opportunity Grant, Julie Bryant and Bill Roach of Playa, Christopher and Marissa North of Almassera Vella, Judith Barrington and Ruth Gundle, and Jim and Margaret Wood for giving me opportunities and support during the period many of these poems were written.

Heartfelt thanks to Atelier 6000's founder and director Pat Clark for honoring these poems with publication both as an art book and as a collection of poetry. Deep appreciation to Ron Schultz who blessed these words with his formidable skills as artist and printmaker. The beauty of the overall design of every aspect of this book, type to lay-out, is thanks to the creative genius of typographers and designers Thomas Osborne and Sandy Tilcock who wove letter and image into a work of graphic beauty.

Thanks to Marianne Borg, David Bong, Mary Evers, Mark Thomas, Ruth Williamson and many others who pointed me toward inspirational writings and perspectives and to Margaret Heater and Cristy Lanfri who provided the encouragement to complete this collection. I especially want to acknowledge and offer my gratitude to Loretta Slepikas, my sister in walking.

My indebtedness and gratitude goes to the Skyhooks poets for their patient review of many of these poems and to the editing provided by poet Cecelia Hagen and copy editor Louise Hawker.

Introduction

Following in the footsteps of thousands of pilgrims, penitents, and seekers over centuries, in 2012 I walked the sacred ground of Spain's *Camino de Santiago* in search of answers to "What's next?" questions, a quest prompted by stepping down after eleven years as founder/director of a literary arts nonprofit. A month spent walking alongside others with their separate sets of petitions, my worldly needs in a backpack, seemed the right prescription for slate-cleaning. It was never my intention to write about my experience, rather, as I walked, to determine which of the writing projects I'd been hungering to begin I'd first tackle on return.

But the list of life questions I was certain I'd resolve while walking the Way was quickly supplanted with what the *Camino* had in mind, including, as it turns out, what I'd write next. When I got back to Oregon and was sorting through brochures and mementos of the trip, I stumbled on a map of the ten *Camino* routes that converge in Santiago. What jumped out at me, looking at that small map, was the stick-figure outline of a woman leaping. In that moment *Camino* Woman was born in my imagination and she wouldn't let me go. She insisted on being written. Fleshing out her fictional character, as the embodiment of all holy women marginalized by patriarchal religions, spawned other characters including a fictionalized *peregrina* "of a certain age", a stylized and profane Catholic church in Father Tomas, an omniscient third-person voice, the role of the *hospitalero* as wisdom keeper, and caricatures of others met along the Way.

The origin of the title? The *Camino de Santiago* is sometimes referred to as the *Vía Láctea*, a reference to the fact that the Milky Way is always overhead when walking the *Camino*. This observation by early day pilgrims inspired the legend that the Milky Way was formed by the dust kicked up by pilgrims' feet. *Vía Láctea* is a verse novel, with a storyline that threads through it. It includes many styles and forms of poetry including free verse, new forms, and traditional ones—such as the haibun, described as terse prose usually ending with a haiku. The haibun is often associated with travel writings, and is sometimes described as a narrative epiphany so it not only suited my style of poetry but also this walk, one that included journaling every day, that is after changing the bandages on my sore feet! The tanka, sometimes referred to as "short song" is best known in its 5/7/5/7/7 syllable count form. Its meter and shape on the page both mimicked the robotic action, day after day, of walk, eat, sleep, walk some more and the isolation I sometimes felt on the trail. Another form was the ghazal, built of couplets and repetitions. Its form mirrored for me the constant rain, day after day, while on the *Camino*. May you enjoy your walk through this staggered telling, this story in poems. *Buen Camino!*

PRE AMBLE

You have not grown old, and it is not too late
to dive into your increasing depths
where life calmly gives out its own secret.

RAINIER MARIA RILKE
from *The Book of Hours*
(translated by Robert Bly)

LATE FALL

This poem is about thin summer dresses wrapped in tissue paper, sweaters
pulled from cedar boxes, studded tires lifted from hooks on the garage
wall. I count to eight when I do everything—pour coffee or whiskey, give
myself a breast exam, get hit in the head lifting studded tires, apply Clarins
concealer #3. This poem is about vacuuming dried cat throw-up from under
my bed and how much I love chocolate.

Just when I think I am on the verge of knowing where home is, I remember
what this poem is about: not knowing; two yellow pears on a leafless tree,
their skin puckered and creped with cold; the cracked egg stuck in the egg tray;
my microwave shorting out, the big noise it made. I was right next to the oven
door when it happened. That was the noise: my heart exploding. My heart cooked
from the inside out. This poem is about which part of all this is fate?

This poem is about the settling of contents. This unsettled poem is about
discontentment. This poem is about the four things each of us settle on
to talk about our whole lives. This poem is about not recognizing anyone
in the room I've been in for 30 years, about my car driving itself to her door
the day she died. It turns out this poem is about stencils. Because I am what
I am and what I'm not.

And when I let myself, I believe love is special and huge and precise and on purpose
but then I remember that if I lived in Randomville I would meet someone there who
wanted to run and jump. This poem is about: there I was thinking about doing certain
things and here I am still thinking about doing certain things, about shrinking possibility,
about spending what I don't have as though that would create it. Is that reckless
or the whole abundant point? This poem is about part of the whole point.

This poem is about blah, blah, my baby kitten, the most embarrassing thing that happened in
high school. This poem is about so sorry, delay, yes, disappointed,however, having said, I am
sure. About the furnace switching on, my house bleeding energy. About raking aspen leaves
that scatter like golden paper coins. When I can't sleep I slip naked into the hot tub. That's
when I remember what this poem is about: the snow-covered bench in the garden, pine cones
from the giant ponderosa knocking across my roof. I call out: *Who's there?*

DREAM CATCHER

I eat standing up because I am about
to be on my way somewhere. I just
know it. I don't sit. The music hasn't
stopped, not yet. And anyway, there's
only one chair and I am the only one
here. I line up *Self, Time, Fortune, Vanity
Fair* edge to edge, tuck hospital corners
on the bed, straighten the Oriental rug—
measures of order to tighten the weave,
to increase the chances of a good thing
catching.

What have I already told you?
That life has more meaning
now that I know it doesn't
than when I thought it did?
Of course, I love life whenever
I can. Or I will. I swear it. Meanwhile
I'll make sure my fork touches
my plate politely. No haste, clatter,
no shove, no scrape—telling
of one who eats alone.

PRE AMBLE

"The Camino is sacred," I'd been told. "Do it when you can." I was ready now. After decades of pretense and puffing up, of climbing the steep curves of learning, I was stepping down. I'd phoenixed before, but how many more fresh starts did I have? Bring on the smudging of miles, the clambering up rocky slopes to knowing *something*. Bring on the clean-slating, the re-grouping, remembering. How far must I go to come home? To be honest, life scares me. Most of the time I feel I'm tumbling in space. The last thing I understand is this so-called state of grace. My children's searing grief. Their holy father's suicide. Our family album? *Guernica* set in the ranching West. Our favorite food group? Post traumatic stress. I try my best because of God's promise.

Be kind and compassionate to my children.
Please, show me that You know them.
I don't mean to be flip. Amen.

There are times I sense the presence of something greater and fall down weeping. I'm not kidding or Catholic. I have never buried Saint Joseph upside down in my garden. (My house sold anyway.) After six Episcopalian decades of confessing, I get it. I've not done those things I ought to. I have done those things I ought not. But, damn it, there is health in me. Plus I keep all lines to the divine mysterious open: meditate before a bronze Buddha, a ceramic Japanese cat, one raised paw petitioning pennies from heaven and, on the occasion of Venus

out-of-bounds, I send a slice of bread down river with my list of wishes wax-sealed inside.

What is my path, my calling?
What is Thy will so I can do it?
If only it worked that way. Amen.

What happens next is I run into a friend (an acquaintance, really) at a party. "You're thinking of doing the Camino? Me too. What a coincidence! I'd planned on going alone but we could go together!" she says. "Why not?" I reply offhandedly. Like it's a day hike. A girlie date for a pedi. *I'd feel braver with somebody*, I think. Some don't make decisions without a cost/benefit analysis, a long list of pros and cons. They've got their top-down convertible IRA to show for it. Not me. I've got a nest without an egg. I'm admired for my willingness to step up, take a swing. I'm at bat again. Only this time it's the top of a late inning.

Dear Maneki-neko, bless me
with a lifetime supply of yen.
This is urgent. Amen.

The two of us didn't realize it, but in that splintered second, I, brooding-seeker, and she, knows-no-strangers, became each other's Siamese twin conjoined at the walking stick, the single purpose, the un-hip, the certainty based on surmise. We signed on to be each other's hostel-mate, looking and shattered glass, unblinking reflection, unholy oil and water; became sisters in wind burn, in forging ahead and friendship.

God comes in many guises. Amen.

POEM.COM

I don't have a poem, only a single line. I've tried
everything: drew words from a hat, set the timer,
but couldn't go deeper than skin; flirted with lines
from notable poets but they left me wanting
or I them; plied villanelles on all fours; rubbed
some bad haiku boys down with scented word oils;
paraded around in one-syllable thongs; but no poem
came. At least not with the power to stay my (dis) course.

So I searched online and found poem.com. Zip coded
possibilities. Shared geographies and longings.
Some wanting phrases, some smoke-stained,
clipped, or druggy, some traditional, rhyming or free,
some flabby, some energetic, some violent, some
gentle, some cowboy. It was a tour of the humane
society for lost lines, truncated iambs peering at me
between the back/slashes of their incomplete life
sentence. Take me home! they seemed to say. I could
identify but not subscribe.

If you were a single line of poetry closing in on *point finale,* would you
still pursue the notion of a couplet, or just give it up once and for all?

THE UNBEARABLE HEAVINESS OF BEING

The guidebook said carry
no more than twelve
percent of your body weight.
I spent a fortune getting
lite. Alice in Caminoland.
Which side of the mushroom
to bite? GoreTex streamline
Ultra Mini quick-wicking
dri proof nano leaves of laundry
soap in a matchbook? Imagine
that. Tiny clothes line, tiny
chamois, panties that dry at the speed
of night, featherweight poncho
in an egg-sized sac, an I-can-take-it
Patagonia jacket that nests in its own
pocket. Smart wool, doll-sized shampoo,
minute head lamp, collapsible sun hat.
Buy, buy, buy. I'm flat and broke before
I start. I don't know jack about knives
or trekking but I'll look the part. I make
my hand into a fist and punch everything
down. Hard. Pull the pack tight shut. Lash
nano sleeping sac, walking sticks to the back.
I strip to my birthday suit, stand on
the bathroom scale with and without
my knapsack. Good news. I make my weight.

But I'm not done yet. What I jam in last
are the heaviest to carry. Zip Loc
bags, ten maybe, labeled in black magic
marker stuffed with muffin-topped vanities
that Spanks don't disguise; issues about aging
that blue eye shadow and rouge belie; silky
scarves, gold rings and other fattening
conceits of pouting privilege wanted but denied;
a poly-unsaturated fear of ordinary; high
sucrose fears of lonely. I hoist the bulging
pack onto my back, cinch the waist and chest straps,
step on the scale. I'm way past my limit.

DISTANT VERIZONS

Before leaving I went looking for truth and
information at Verizon; asked Brad, according
to his badge, to explain the apps and options I could
not fathom, but mine by virtue of owning a phone
with smarts. Thankfully, Brad, handsome and strong,
was the expert on the symbols floating on the glassy
flatness, mysterious hieroglyphs depicting worlds I couldn't
imagine...I, like some time-traveling aboriginal, more
comfortable with clay tablets than this space-age gadget.
Brad, when I go, how will it know?

To show me, he delicately traces one thick finger across
the smooth surface; taps lightly on an icon like a gentle
colossus knocking on a tiny door; tilts the glistening
wafer ever so slightly, so none of the symbols slide off
the doll-sized platter. In Brad I see a new and wondrous species
of man, the very kind I long for, one capable of infinitesimal
and tender gestures. I feel suddenly hopeful about peace,
prosperity in the whole world... "Ma'am," Brad interrupts
my reverie, "it wants you to say a command."

ARTIFICIAL CONNECTIONS

When I was little my father called me Bubble
because in the bath tub I was scared I'd pop, disappear
down the gargling maw when my mother removed
the rubber stopper. It's the same now as I pull the plug
on work, empty the porcelain hold of house, breach
the levee of living virtually. Re-tired, -treaded, -cycled.
What is left of me? This question isn't new. Maybe
I'll learn to take comfort in the shared invisibility
among the, go ahead, say it, female elderly. I doubt it.

Stripped of power, I light a candle to read the wishes
I pencil in the thinning margins of time. Goals, bucket
lists. Asking who I am in act three might seem a bit late.
So. I'm a late bloomer. I'll take what I can get and a long
walk through Spain. I've disconnected from the drain
of the stasis of being, too many outlets, sockets, boosters,
miseri cords, voice recorders, black box. What will I say
when I go down for good? Skid marks on the tarmac
of my last testament. What I will and won't. Advance
the directive. This life of mine is still mine. What of it?

EXIT ROW

I like this lofty world of the exit row, air-
borne, not stuck in perpetual utero tight
within earth's restraining sac where the end
of the story is implicit in its confining shape
and mine.

For a life among the clouds, read the placard,
says the angel of the skies, small golden wings
springing from her breast. She models low
and tight, flotation, oxygen; reminds
that the hardest landings happen below.

This suited seraph touches down on the aftermath
of crashes, grief, maintenance records. At last
count untold numbers impacted by death, the shrapnel
scattered for lives. All this mortality renders me
queasy, my big ideas like scarves lifting in silky
pallor, drawn through the ceiling vent to land
as ghosts, much later, along the frozen road
thousands of feet below.

PASSPORT

STAMPED ENTRY: *April 3, 2012. Madrid Barujas. Temporary.* I already know about the limited term of stay but it bears repeating.

NAME: *Ellen Waterston.* Hovering above the choppy waters I search for a landing drawn by the rosined bow of a father's cello, scored with the keys of his late night typing; a place x'd with crimson stain from a mother's reluctant womb, a uterine palette that bled watercolors and India ink. All the beauty and love I've known is sizedwith salt tears.

PERMISSION TO PROCEED: I finally understand. Now was always the time.

DESTINATION: *Hostel el Pilar, Madrid.* From the back seat of the pressing yellow taxi, past the right ear of the silent driver, I see ecstatic throngs flushed with religious fervor. *Semana de Pascua.* Processions fill the streets. The crypt. The knock. God answers for His Son. The Holy Virgin answers for Her Son. The Son answers for His Parents.It's a mystery, this three in one. Ornate biers supported on the shoulders of the faithful *costalleros* sway down cobbled streets. Men in masks and pointed hats flank the weeping Madonna, the crucified Jesus; play a rabid, bloody dirge on dented trumpets, small, tinny drums. I hit the ground walking.

CAMINANTE

To regret that something wasn't started sooner only delays its beginning.

HUGH PRATHER

CAMINO WOMAN I: LEAPING PETROGLYPH

I am a leaping petroglyph, my she-shape traced
by the feet of centuries of praying pilgrims
filing across the rocky face of Galicia. My limbs
are sketched by the ten *caminos*. My stick figure
legs straddle Spain, the thin train of my dress
trails careless over the Pyrenees into France. One
of my olive-groved arms plumbs Portugal, the barnacled
other breakwaters the coast of *Mar Cantábrico*.
Tied in eucalyptus, my long graying braids, *Primitivo*,
Plata, dangle across each of my mossy, cobblestone breasts.
No matter which way pilgrims choose—
Portugués,
del Norte,
Fisterra-Muxia,
de la Plata,
Aragonés,
Inglés,
Sanabrés
Podiensis,
Primitivo,
Francés
—no matter which god they falsify, in the end it is my clay flesh,
my coursing waters that lead them to Santiago's doorway of glory.

FATHER TOMAS I: CATHOLIC JACKPOT

Hello! Greetings. Come in! Come in! Before you start walking, *peregrinos* and *peregrinas,* let me bless your pilgrimage. Right this way into my church, the cathedral of *Pulchra Leonina.* Only a moment of your time. My prayer for you: believe in something outside of self. You'll feel better. It's the best antidote to the absurdity of your life. Personally I recommend our Savior Jesus Christ. Of all the plans, the options, it's the best coverage. Three for the price of one. How do you do? I'm Father Tomas.

Today's special noon-time bonanza mass includes kissing the alabaster feet of Jesus and another chance to pull down on the lever of blind faith. Watch the boys' chorus line up to sing. Relish their honeyed sound. The lights are low. No day or night in this sacred place. No clocks. Eternity is the only time worth keeping. Take wafer, wine, kneel with the weary working men and women. They cross themselves, queue up, touch their pursed lips to the tip of the holy big toe. Then, penitent, they go to their pews to empty their pockets of prayers into the metaphysical slot machine.

They know if they play according to the rules of tithe and devotion, sometimes supplications of like color and shape align. Then the golden cascade of good fortune echoes in the gaming cathedral. Their children succeed, arthritis goes away, the backyard chickens all lay an egg simultaneously the very same day. You too can play and pray, my *peregrinos.* True. Some leave downcast, empty of prayer and pocket. I remind them life is the gamble. God is not. After mass I serve hot soup in the rectory, for some the closest thing that day, that year, maybe ever, to experiencing His love.

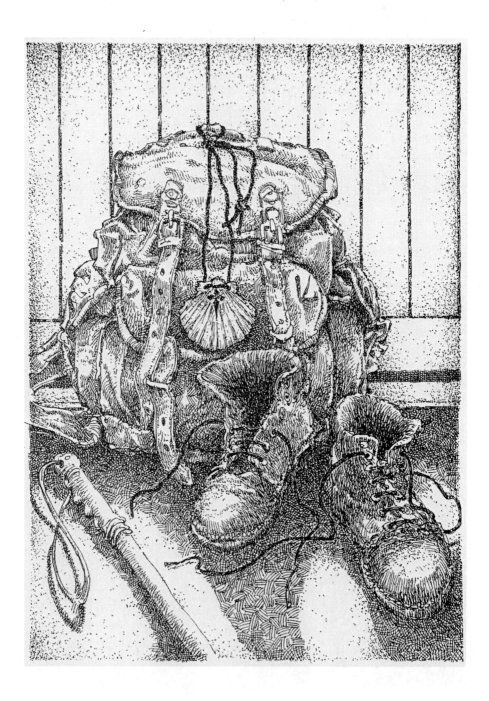

CAMINO WOMAN 2: FROM MY BELLY

The blade of Saint James' cross
brights red on the scallop shell lashed
to the *peregrina's* pack the day she starts
the trek in León. From my belly she springs,
half way along the *Camino Francés*. She begins
walking. Walking. She is walking, starting
at my navel, belayed by my umbilical cord down
the sheer face of her seeking. There she is alone
and together with all pilgrims over centuries.

I AM WALKING

And what of the ultimate peace that passes all understanding? John Brierley

Registered, picked up my *credencia* and pilgrim's scallop shell at Plaza de Santa Maria. The brown robed *hospitalero* named the three stages of the *Camino:* exhilaration, pain, surrender. Can't Catholics count past trinity? "I plan to skip the last two," I said. He smiled knowingly.

Stage one crash-landed after only four of the Brierley guidebook's 20-plus mile days. My feet are bloody, blistered. My body's too heavy to carry. I lighten my load, discard things I can't live without. I'm not down with Brierley's prescriptions for personal reflection.

Hard to know what I really feel with so much commentary, direction. Noisy. Like the TV's in every bistro. Who is this *señor* guidebook busybody? All Q, no A. Aspects of self, You say? (Who's that talking to me?)

Me, myself and I—unholy trio, more toe to toe, mano à mano, than eye to eye. I move "Change your attitude" to the top of my prayer list. Maybe that's the whole point of this. I can go home now. I wish.

Saw another *peregrina* in a café, a woman my age I'd guess. She lowered her head to her plate to eat. She had given up. I told myself if you must be old sit up straight, shoulders back, don't breathe through your mouth, cover your yawns, don't drool or snore or talk to yourself.

It's raining again and again.

Heel, toe, blisters scream.
I can barely take a step.
Where does the Way lead?

Forget God, speed. Give
me Compeed band-aids filled
with air, blister care.

CAMINO WOMAN 3: TATTING

This particular *peregrina*. She calls
her first day "beginning." She'll see.
There is no such thing. So earnest,
she presses her self-important prayers
between her palms, into the ground
beneath the insistent beat of her calloused,
screaming feet. Soon her shins will be
splintering. The olive oil, the wine,
the blood of the butchered pig, the muttered,
pitted prayers of those who've gone
before laugh and weep for her. Because
the answer is always the same. Few see,
so fascinated with their own tatting. This one
no exception. Oh, the elaborate filigree
of this *peregrina's* needs. Who does she think
she is? Do I tell her now, so soon in the telling?
No. The time will come to show there is no power
or plan hers alone. I will meet her in Manjarin.

In the farmer's field
A stork is hunting green frogs.
May the Way be blessed.

STORK

The lean of my long-necked

    strut, my back-bending-not-knee

and beady eye. Preening, lauding

    one-legged over my straw hat nest,

rakish on bell tower, feeding greedy

    young, the clamor and clack. Now,

slow-motion I lift my whole feather,

    bill, hollow-boned beauty, deftly tuck

my walking stilts under prehistoric wings,

    hatching the skyway white and black

with the action of my ponderous flight.

    At night I transport the dead on my back

to heaven, in my beak carry babies

    to the barren. Sunrise, I spot the sweets

on the sill of your longing and come

    to fledge your foundling prayers.

TWO HOTS AND A COT

cold rain dark
must stop
twelve Euros
two hots a cot
I'll take it
sello red-inked
stamped steeple-
shape fits the square
on pilgrim
credencial
twenty
in one room
men women
claim cots
check for bed
bug blood
spots
bodily
smells sounds
piss wash
menu fixed
to bed on tip
toe
stuff
pillow
with what
can't afford
to lose
snore squalls ear
plugs
up early in dark
line up naked
concrete
block
shower room cold
quick dry
repack
toast coffee grab
sticks walking
before sunrise

WHY ARE YOU WALKING?

Harold, Herman, Elena, Adolpho, Ulf, Beatrice, Valdir,
Leopold, Isidro, Yang, Franz, Christopher, Nicholas, Barbara,
Marc, Graeme, Manual, Raj, Erik, Annick, Lisa, Tu.

My marriage is a lie/ I think I'm gay/my wife died/no reason/
there's so much to be thankful for/ here with my grandchildren/
have cancer/distributing my father's ashes/addict in recovery/going
blind/daughter committed suicide/save the planet/just for fun/
find purpose/ make friends/seek forgiveness/enlightenment/new
beginning/find laughter/find a lover/too fat/celebrate life/pray for
peace/escape loneliness/practice joy/be seen/be unseen/understand
death/praise God/find God/rediscover wonder/remember

CAMINO WOMAN 4: THE PATH

There is no cure for living. Except
to walk. In time with your life. The path
the *peregrina* seeks, her very own, is made
by walking. Nothing more. Her footsteps
are the path. The path is made by walking.
Her footsteps are the path.

(After a poem by Antonio Machada)

CLOTHESLINE AT THE HOSTEL

On a day of partial sun I hang my underwear
next to the hostel's dishtowels on the democratic
line. Whatever my delicates' true feelings, they,
uncomplaining, share clothespins with other pilgrims'
stained socks, halter tops nipped at the nape,
pick-pocketed quick-wicking trousers strung up
by the cuffs and shirts, shoulders pinched into a shrug
against unseasonal cold. Black panties are pinned
next to the gaping bravado of a stranger's unbuttoned
boxers or tee-shirts' rude homilies for living, turned
upside down. Bras with lace trim fill slightly
in the wind, a tutorial in caress. Sleep sacs luff, breathe
the sweet smell of line-dried. Some pins, unemployed,
dangle on the fraying nylon cord, others lie shattered
in the dirt, silver spring corkscrewing uselessly
next to the broken finger of the wooden pincer.

ANGELS OF REJECTION

Forgiveness is giving up that the path could be different.

VALERIE HARPER

TRESPASS

Space-docking with strangers along the way. Hummingbird encounters. Best friends just met. False glee. Chit-chat. Is that a corn silo? See the church, see the steeple, open the door, take a photo. I distance myself. Take a second look. Vines suckle depleted soil. Turbines crowd out the feral boar. Nothing wild. Nothing sings. The *Camino* clings to lines of power that scar the hills. Cities' yellow pallor sickens the sun. Sour air clogs my lungs. Crucifixes made of twigs are splayed on a wire fence, tumbleweed prayers hanging on barbless hope. Along the road a child's crib, a broken plate, and, descending into Trabadelo, a naked mannequin, feet amputated at the ankle.

farmer with cows stops
tourists trespass with snap shots
woman herding sheep
weeps behind her parasol
pilgrims endured, cash crop
villagers reduced to props

VÍA LÁCTEA

It's said the Milky Way's but dust kicked up
by pilgrims' feet, the wheel-shaped star-city made
by *peregrinos* walking. The shimmering arrow
of Sagittarius points to the middle of the misty
arch where sparkles and flares blend in giant curved
arms of gleam and Camino powder.

The Sun teeters on the edge of this spiral fanfare,
fancying our distant world with ancient light
where luminous bands of the religious walk the trail
of ghosts in clusters, chains, ribbons. Each pilgrim
part of the same spiral story; each pilgrim's prayer,
a pinprick in the bag of obsidian night, writing
a new, bright galactic star-way, illuminating
the raven abyss.

But heed this, the tongue of the galaxy grows thick
with time and distance. Less and less intelligible,
depleted Jovian giants bellow across light years.
They say: Wake from your arrogance, your tumbling
sleep, lest your El Niño oceans boil. Beware the outrush
of expanding notions of self, the rapacious black hole
of your greed. Even the present night is eclipsed by day.

CAMINO WOMAN 5: APOCRYPHA

is the god you pray to   pretty, male and white
come back to me   hurry, before it's too late
if not   there will be
ruin   nothing left of earth, mankind
I was here before   this penial trinity
birth   requires a woman
and so with rebirth   a fertile womb
this   the original order
Nature imbued   with sacred Spirit
ignore   me
at your peril   defy
those   misogynists
who deny   the she-sun
would chop   down
the Tree of Life   destroy
He/She   divine unity

FATHER TOMAS II: ORIGINAL SIN

man's savage

      nature must be confined

temptations

      removed

there is none greater than

      woman

her original sin

      condemns us to

pudendal hell

      seek knowledge of God

in its purest form

      feelings of lust have no place

CHILL

Don't the others see
her sitting at this table
alone and eager
for a deep conversation?
The Brazilian is flirting

with her walking friend.
The young Italian woman
passes her over,
favoring noisy chatter
at the next table's far end.

She could go join them.
But they are drunk on so much
frivolity; talk
only of aches, clothing, rain,
kilometers left to walk.

She's here on business,
to ask big questions, to make
a plan for what's left
of her life, to give it some
relative meaning, purpose,

to get quiet, still.
It's hard work, at times lonely.
She's chilled to the bone.
There is warmth in their laughter.
There is warmth in their laughter.

NEIN, DANKE

With my small change
I buy you a latte.
My seductive stare
licks
the froth off
your spoon.
I invite you
to my so-so private
room. Maybe
my timing is
good today? I am
Harold *von* Munich.
You seem wanting
a friend along the Way
so, as I say, you are
beautiful. You will
believe me
if you're not in
your skin, if
you still think
it is for someone else
to put you in.
A common condition
among lost or aging
women. I am here
to oblige
but we must hurry
before my wife
Skypes me.
Und so, und so ...
No? *Ach!* This one
a waste of my money.
No matter. There are
so many.

RAIN

The dark skies suggested the potential for rain.
The belief was it would be light, seasonal rain.

But daily it pounds the tile roofs, crofts and hedge rows.
Nothing escapes the torrential rain.

Cobblestoned streets weep with manure. The backs
of animals steam in the rain.

Shrouded in ponchos we look like specters,
the ghouls of perpetual rain.

Dripping down our necks, soaking socks and gloves,
the downpour has virtual reign.

We slog mile after muddy mile
through the unfathomable rain.

The pain in our feet is inconsequential
compared to the persistent rain.

We shield our faces from wind and pellets,
against the hail and Mary of all rains.

I'd counted on sunlit joy but learn to find it
in the baptismal rain.

HOSPITALERO RX

I heard the man complain you stood in the way of the fire. And you moved, as though he had special claim. You forget there is no limit to the supply of Spirit and you are deserving of it. As to the boisterous *peregrino,* as though the only one with hurting feet? As designated healer, I've got time and cleanser enough for all. Life has been hard? I'm sorry, truly, but compared to what? Life's *camino* gives you what you need. Here's the invitation: with this ragged band of strangers, across the rugged miles ahead, listen to the language of your prayers. Worry is praying for what you don't want. What you believe, you attract. Simple as that.

Now, before soup, bread, and a cot, come rest your leg on my brown-robed lap. My long beard tickles your toes. Ha, ha! I hold each foot in my spider fingers, peer at your blisters through spectacles on the end of my hawk-like nose. I singe the sewing needle in the blue of the candle's flame, poke the hot point into the puss-filled vesicle, premature pop, induced labor, hastened birth of transformation, oozing release, then the stinging benediction of Betadine. Each pustule a regret let go. Laugh at the pain! Bless each abscess. Walk slowly. You can't storm heaven. God's speed is not fast.

The shuttered dark room
feels like a coffin. Airless.
I the cadaver.

ALADDIN'S LAMP

I'll tell you three things about me. Only one is not true.
1.
2.
3.

I get three wishes?
1.
2.
3.

Here are three things I believe:
1.
2.
3.

DOGS OF FONCEBADON

Ridge line leading to the Iron Cross traced by snarling shadows. Dingos, feral dogs

Eye me, sullen trot, stop, lift their leg to steam-seal the frozen boundaries of my purgatory.

Guttural growl, fur bristling behind their anvil heads, they

Rush at my hastening heels, fangs bared in a wolfish grin, sinister,

Excited by the stench of rancid remorse. I stop, suddenly mighty,

Turn, meet their carnivorous stares, pick up a rock, slung, shot, another, another,

Striking dead-on turned-tails, whimpering exiles. The panting ghost pack vanishes into the hills.

ANGELS
OF JOY

If we're not supposed to dance, why all this music?

GREGORY ORR

CRUZ DE FERRO

She left three stones
from her volcanic home
on the cold mountain
pumice for lightness
on the cold mountain
obsidian for right action
smoky crystal for wisdom
on the cold mountain

She could finally cry,
say goodbye to him
on the cold mountain

Could praise Father robed
in purple heather, Great Mother
in the extravagant weather
on the cold mountain

All sadness was lifted,
forgiveness gifted
on the cold mountain

She saw her children
and theirs, swaddled
them in prayers
on the cold mountain

She would carry them
to Finisterre over any
cold mountain

CAMINO WOMAN 6: MEETING AT MANJARIN

To everyone I offer the map of my body. Few see it, but you did. Braids gray, dingy. My smile glint-toothed. My limbs lithe, leathery. I am centuries old. My pelvis cradles the cosmic womb. I feed on exiled stones, apples, radiance, coal and pearls. I drink from the chalice of the voice of the dove. I am the Great Goddess, the sensate Mary, the burning center, the divine spouse in sacred union with the ground, the invisible within. I am all God's holy women banished by men.

Part the string of tattered, flapping prayers. Enter my secret palace, this mystical garden of Eden, my sacred warren of candle-lit altars. You heard, inside cold stone barns, the knocking bells around the necks of steaming cows, in the copse, the cuckoo's smoky signal calling all my names. And you came and found me at Manjarin.

For you I light the essence of time, the incense of the infinite. I make your body ache until you forget your list of petty petitions. Stop pacing the confining halls of your worries, reducing the magnificence of the world to your carefully arranged concerns. Fall out of love with your sad story. Be a hero in your flawed journey. You will be alive 1,000 years from now. Live that way. Who will you tell? Few will listen. Fewer will hear.

MILAGROS

There's no breeze but the curtain lifts.

My dead father waves from the farmhouse window.

The giantess living on holy dirt flies next

to me, breathes a long, loud haaah warm

on my neck.

      What you believe, you will find

      your revelation there. If it is doubt, then doubt

      is where. If evil, then there. If unbelief, know it

      as magnificent.

GATES OF FORGIVENESS

I unlist, undo, immaculately re-conceive. I am in a dream. In the dream

     I am walking.

In the dream I walk for a living. In the dream I meet

     the Camino Woman. I wake up and leave the land of why, enter

the land of now. The left hand of lightness, the right hand of both/and.

     I make time

at the rate of forgiveness. Today, God is in my sore hip, God

     is in this rest day, hot bath, oxtail stew, garlic *pulpo*. God is in the orange cat lazy

by the door to the milk shed, the red chickens scratching in the leaves.

FATHER TOMAS III: PRAYER REQUEST

An unseasonal snowstorm. You poor pilgrims. In my limo I passed you trudging to
O'Cebreiro. God asks a lot of some. It could be worse. Those ancient thatched *pallozas*
were all that sheltered pilgrims of old. Brrr. I'm glad for my wool coat. What an elegant,
small cathedral, no? Come in. Mass begins. I want to show you something. No, God no, not
all those naked *putti* on the domed ceiling like a bucket full of seething chum. Rather, an
exciting innovation, the modernization of God.

I sit here by the altar in a red velvet chair, I operate the remote, project slides of the beautiful
Jesus: in a loin cloth, thin, pale, bearded, rosy, a boy, a man, crucified, risen, in Technicolor,
infused with artificial light. Powerpoint Jesus. Translated five ways. Systems of delivery.
Catholic marketing strategy. To bring you closer to Him. Sing along:

*Captain of the heavens, this is my prayer request. You don't have to grant it but I hope You'll
do your best. I've been watching Your show on the video and You seem like my God to me.*

*confused old farmer
stands, his back to the altar
looking for the door*

STREET BAND

We've been laid off by the Ford plant
in Valencia, all of us here in the same
fix. Here's what we do about it. Walk
the *Camino*, kiss the crucifix, offer song
and thanks. I blow my brass whistle, one,
two, raise my walking stick. My six friends
and I, our own *Camino* street band.

We parade joyous through the sleet and fog,
skip, prance, tumble with laughter, shape
and throw soft balls of snow at one another.
The weathervane turning in the wind stops
and points to right now. I perfectly greet you.
I perfectly rejoice in the rain. Today I dine
on *pulpo* and wine and it is perfect.

WAYMARKERS

Life don't easy. Sheila

Lose the life you think you're supposed to live. Hugh Prather

Pain is inevitable, suffering is optional. Haruki Murakami

We are only as happy as our least happy child. Eliot

Let life bounce you back. Sam

God is in the hunch that keeps coming up when you get quiet. Jon

Don't look where you don't want to go. Dave

Marry me, Lisa Left. Graeme

We're here to help each other get through this, whatever it is. Mark Vonnegut

No vino, no *Camino*. Harold

THE
END
OF
THE
EARTH

And, in that place to which your best dreams take you, there are those who have been waiting ...

JOHN CULKIN

FATHER TOMAS IV: WHAT ON EARTH WILL HAPPEN

Blessings! You made it to Santiago! Come, come,
into the cathedral. Today as *tiraboleiro*, I
will help celebrate the Pilgrim's Mass. Look
for me in my red robe, pulling the cord
of the *bota*. The glistening canister slowly swings
through the apse, contrails of cleansing
incense fumigate the sins of those gathered. Soon
the momentum of the arcing censer lifts me
onto the toes of my shiny black shoes.

The thurible swings higher. I pull, release the white silk rope,
working with the contractions of your confessions, the push
of your prayers. The fuming orb rises toward the ceiling,
sweeps me off my feet. I am flying, gliding past murals
of heaven, stained glass saints, the light of God shining
through them, at me, at me.

Now I careen wildly toward a mosaic
of Mary. Her arms reach out to embrace me.
"No!" I cry, a peterless Pan as I shatter through the blue
glass folds of the Magdalene. It's then I plead
my confession: I have not loved all of God's creation,
my sisters as myself. Open the doors of glory
to all women. Yes! Let the fiesta begin. Only God
can know what on earth will happen.

CAMINO WOMAN 7: YOU ARE THE THANK YOU

Enter the gaudy cathedral of Santiago,
the faceted chambers of the grand jewel
that decorates my throat. Can you find me
in the gilded noise? Press your brow against
the head of *Santo d'os Croques* and receive
the miracle imprint of my red bindi.

Doubters moan, their wails ricochet off the ribs
of the basilica, this monument to institutionalized
hope. They suffer the sting of clinging to their
personalized prayers. But you. Get up off your knees,
step out into the day. You now are the thank you,
the world is your welcome.

FINISTERRE

A child playing in the sand at Willow
Dell watches a faraway ship fall
off the edge of the earth. To explain,
her father holds up an orange, traces
its girth, his finger reappearing like
a pale sun cresting a citrus world.

Since Domini began, penitents have crawled
on their knees to the ocean-swept cliffs
of Finisterre, apprehending the distant
horizon to be earth's end. Chastened,
they returned to their towns, a fluted shell
proof of bearing witness to the absolute.

This modern-day *peregrina* stands at water's
edge, looks across the Bay of Biscay where
the horizon of her life intersects with the void.
What false endings does she believe, what limits
of nature, of being? The eternal tide washes
over the shore, an orange sun slips
behind a receding world.

TIME WARP

Some would say I did things half way because I didn't start at the beginning in Saint-Jean-Pied-de-Port, (on the French side of the Pyrenees). What I know now, that I didn't before, is that all I can do is start at my beginning, go to my end, and then stop.

My *credencial* cascades open across the counter like a Jacob's Ladder, the endless climb to heaven folding in on itself. The clerk at Santiago inspects my stamps, verifies I have gone the requisite distance, presents me with an official certificate of pilgrimage. Of the forty squares, I filled thirty-six. I ask him: "If the *credencial* is my life span, how much time do I have left?"

At Finisterre I encountered a pilgrim doing what the ancients did. After washing his face in the Bay of Biscay he turned to go back to where he started. I realized then infinity is what the Camino describes, the ellipsis, the oval track, the overlapping figure eight of the Milky Way that we all walk endlessly.

The man waiting ahead of me to board the plane back to the United States wears a T-shirt that says: *There is no finish line.*

The beginning of
the end, the end of the beginning,
world without end. Amen.

NOVEMBER SUN—

flower stands like stork, stubborn on one thin yellowed

      stalk, serrated head slung slack, hangman's fracture.

Her beaded orb cast downward, spent seeds tumble groundward

from its single round eyeball, intent on one socket of dirt in front

      of its craned pencil foot, as if sheer-willing pods

of unfinished flower business beneath insulating leaf, mud, snow –

so that patiently, later, not now, when March looses the gelid hold, first stirs

      the buried, soggy resolve, when all that's left

of the brittle-maned lioness is rotted, crumpled humus, this hunched

Cyclops will have stared down the earth and won

      the right to another round.

INHALING HOPE

She twists the ribbons tied to the balloons
around her wrist, walks the bright blue
and green Mylar stars and globes outside,
away from the music, into the brisk darkness.
They chafe to fly, despite the cool,
the dwindling light.

Venturing deeper into the night, she looks
to the sky for consolation, listens for the sound
she's told lies beyond silent prayer. Before letting
go the giddy airships, she inhales the helium
of hope, giggles like a hyena. One by one
the balloons disappear from sight.

WHAT I AM GOING TO DO NOW

It's clear the distant
calibrated steppes
are the wiser course,
but for the why not,
the I dare you
of the solitary,
yam-bright willow,
its roots barely
grazing the surface
of the mud flat, branches
heedless, hoping skyward.

MAKE BELIEVE

you're an envelope
with a note inside written
in the form of a prayer.
The all of you, your em—
dash laugh, your run-on
mistakes, is the inscription
written by the Poet in an elegant
metaphysical hand, then folded,
placed inside the envelope that is
you, and gently mailed into the world
when you are born.

Your prayer is written within
the within of you. The space
between each you-word
is where heaven abides. Petitioning
a distant deity is a waste of time.
Prayer is a reporting, a telling.
Every day, if you can, turn more
and more inside-out so the you-
prayer is exposed to more and more light.

ELLEN WATERSTON

Vía Láctea is award-winning author and poet Ellen Waterston's third collection of poetry. She is also the author of a collection of essays and a memoir. She founded the Writing Ranch in 2000 which offers retreats and workshops for emerging writers. She is the founder and former director of The Nature of Words, a literary nonprofit. She lives and writes in Bend, Oregon.

RON SCHULTZ

Ron Schultz's engravings, lithographs and etchings have been exhibited extensively in California and Oregon and are included in many private collections. He has also worked as a book illustrator, landscape designer, technical illustrator, and graphic artist. He currently instructs printmaking at Atelier 6000 in Bend, Oregon.

ATELIER 6000

Atelier 6000 is a nonprofit studio specializing in original prints and book arts. Located in Bend, Oregon's Old Mill District, Atelier 6000 has been in operation since 2007. The studio is dedicated to advancing printmaking and book arts as contemporary art forms. Support from private foundations, corporate giving programs, government programs, and generous individuals helps make the publication of Atelier 6000's books possible.

This perfect bound edition is the companion to a limited edition art book hand-printed by Sandy Tilcock at lone goose press, Eugene Oregon. For information please visit www.atelier6000.org.

Atelier 6000 books are available at:
Atelier 6000, 389 Scalehouse Court, Bend, Oregon 97702
Email: A6@atelier6000.org
Telephone: 541.330.8759

VÍA LÁCTEA

This book is a story told through a number of poetic forms that seamlessly carried me along the *Camino de Santiago*. The narrative pulls readers along, yet the poetry insists that they linger with the music of words and the often-surprising images. In a time when paths and "old ways" are the subject of much writing, Ellen Waterston has found an entirely new way to record her footsteps as they seek out a new direction in her modern life, even while following old traditions. A free-thinker, she is respectful but independent of the Catholicism all around her; honest about her own lack of clarity, she is able to find humor as well as pain in the sometimes grueling task of putting one blistered foot in front of the other. Those who don't usually seek out poetry will find this a compelling read, while those who do will appreciate the craft and creative innovation.

—*Judith Barrington*
Judith Barrington is the author of three volumes of poetry. A fourth, *The Conversation*, is forthcoming in 2015.

In this original and mesmerizing work, we join with author and poet Ellen Waterston in a dance chiaroscuro, spiraling heavenward, stirring the dust of the pilgrim's path on the *Camino de Santiago*. This stunning collection of poetic forms rhythmically and lyrically, give movement to this fine work of art and reflection of a seeker for whom there is no cure except to walk. By embarking on this literary and spiritual path before you, the *Vía Láctea*, you too consent to undergo the three stages of the Camino itself: exhilaration, pain, surrender. With enviable and original skill Waterston articulates in image and form, shade and light, insight and honesty a way that itself is a means of "illuminating the raven abyss." Her journey at once destined and random is "exposed to more and more light"; so is the way when we walk in time with our life.

—*Marianne Borg*
An Episcopal priest, Borg is founding director of The Center for Spiritual Development, an outreach educational ministry of Trinity Episcopal Cathedral, Portland Oregon. After 18 years at the Cathedral she recently retired to Central Oregon where she continues her ministry of spiritual formation, teaching, leading retreats and pilgrimage.

Ellen Waterston is our guide, our pilgrim, our compass through these beautiful and human poems. One feels as if you are walking next to the poet, your heart full—the sky all starlight.

—*Matthew Dickman*
Matthew Dickman is the author of *All-American Poem, Mayakovsky's Revolver,* and co-author of *50 American Plays.*

"We all walk endlessly," states the *peregrina*, the seeker whose voice begins and ends this Chaucerian tale told in an impressive array of forms. Ellen Waterston calls on many voices to recount a *Camino* pilgrimage—voices that offer wit and satire, voices that prickle with gritty observation, voices profane and sacred. One is the embodiment of the female principle. In place of the archetypal Cosmic Man who contains all men, the poet gives her readers Camino Woman, an entity composed from countless women pilgrims—those too long discounted by patriarchal orthodoxy. Another notable voice, the compassionate *hospitalero*, urges the peregrina to "...listen to the language of your prayers." And the *peregrina*—in *Vía Láctea's* final poem—responds: "Petitioning/a distant deity is a waste of time./Prayer is a reporting, a telling..." Indeed, Waterston tells her tale eloquently by speaking to us in the language of poems.

—*Paulann Petersen*
Paulann Petersen is the Oregon Poet Laureate and author of *Understory.*

ISBN 978-0-9893951-1-3

ISBN 978-0-9893951-1-3

$16.50

Tugboat Stories

George Matteson